IRIS
Folding
for Celebrations

Maruscha Gaasenbeek
Tine Beauveser

FORTE PUBLISHERS

Contents

Fifth printing, October 2005
ISBN 90 5877 403 1

This is a publication from
Forte Publishers BV
P.O. Box 1394
3500 BJ Utrecht
The Netherlands

For more information about the creative books available from Forte Uitgevers:
www.forteuitgevers.nl

Editor: Marianne Perlot
Final editing: Hanny Vlaar, Hilversum, the Netherlands
Photography and digital image editing: Fotografie Gerhard Witteveen, Apeldoorn, the Netherlands
Cover and inner design: Bade creatieve communicatie BV, Baarn, the Netherlands
Translation: Michael Ford, TextCase, Hilversum, the Netherlands

Preface

Everyday envelope paper and a simple folding technique form the irresistible combination which everybody knows as Iris folding. The real fans of this technique now use many different types of paper, because the more colours and patterns you have, the more choice you have and the more exciting the end result, the Iris folding card, will be. One card can be bright with strong colours and the next can have lovely soft shades, so that every card is your own unique design. The colour of the card you stick the Iris folding card onto is important, of course, but so is the quality, because when you stick the Iris folding card onto it, the slight difference in height created by the strips must be bridged. The attractive textures make the end result even more appealing. Sometimes, you may even find it difficult to give the cards to other people.

For the patterns in this new book, we let our imagination run wild with the theme **festive days**. We hope that the original patterns will inspire you to make some splendid cards.

Let us celebrate together with our book **Iris Folding for Celebrations**.

Kind regards,

Maruscha   *Tine*

Thanks: Els, Frederique and the other members of the team.

Techniques

The starting point for Iris folding is the pattern. Cut the outline of the pattern out of the back of your card and then fill the hole from the outside to the inside with folded strips of paper. You work at the back of the card, so you work, in fact, on a mirror image. When you have finished the Iris folding, stick the card onto another card. For a hexagonal shape, select six different sheets of paper where the patterns and colours combine and contrast each other nicely. Cut all the paper into strips in the same way, for example, from left to right. The number of different strips you will need depends on the pattern; you will need between four and eight strips. The width of the strips also depends on the pattern and is stated for each card. You need to first fold the edge of the strips over and then sort them into the different colours. Next, cover each section in turn by following the numbers (1, 2, 3, 4, 5, etc.), so that the pattern is continuously rotated. Lay the strips down with the fold facing towards the middle of the pattern and stick the left and right-hand sides to the card using adhesive tape. Finally, use an attractive piece of holographic paper to cover the hole in the middle.

The basic pattern – The hexagon
(see the bottom right-hand corner of page 5 and card 1 on page 9)

The most important thing is to start with the basic pattern, because from this, you will learn the unique folding and sticking technique needed for all the patterns. You will notice that you quickly get used to the technique of Iris folding.

Preparation
1. Lay a piece of ice blue card (13 x 9.7 cm) down with the back facing towards you.
2. With the aid of a light box, draw the outline of the hexagon onto the card using a pencil and cut it out.
3. Stick a copy of the hexagon shown in this book (pattern 1) to your cutting mat using adhesive tape.
4. Place the card with the hole on the pattern (you should be looking at the back of the card) and only stick the left-hand side of the card to your cutting mat using masking tape.
5. Select six different sheets of paper. Two blue envelopes and four sheets of Iris folding paper have been used for the card in the bottom right-hand corner of page 5.
6. Cut 2 cm wide strips from these sheets and make separate piles of colour A, colour B, colour C, colour D, colour E and colour F.
7. Fold the edge of each strip over (approximately 0.7 cm wide) with the nice side facing outwards.

1. More than 650 different insides of envelopes together with Iris folding paper.

2. Cut the hexagon out of the back of a piece of card. Cut the Iris folding paper and the envelopes into strips and fold the edge over.

3. Stick the pattern to your cutting mat. Place the card on top and tape the left-hand side to the cutting mat. Place the fold of the strips exactly against the line and stick down the left and right-hand sides using adhesive tape.

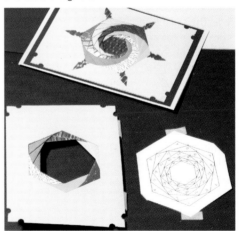

4. Fold the card open from time to time to see whether the patterns continue nicely.

Iris folding

8. Take a folded strip of colour A and place it over section 1, exactly against the line of the pattern with the folded edge facing towards the middle. Allow 0.5 cm to stick out on the left and right-hand sides and cut the rest off. By doing so, the strip will also slightly stick out over the edge of the pattern at the bottom, so that section 1 is totally covered.

9. Stick the strip to the card on the left and right-hand sides using a small piece of adhesive tape, but remain 0.5 cm from the edge of the card.

10. Take a strip of colour B and place it on section 2 of the pattern. Tape the left and right-hand sides to the card.

11. Take a strip of colour C. Place this on section 3 and stick it into place.

12. Take a strip of colour D. Place this on section 4 and stick it into place.

13. Take a strip of colour E. Place this on section 5 and stick it into place. Finally, take a strip of colour F and stick it onto section 6.

14. Continue with colour A on section 7, colour B on section 8, colour C on section 9, colour D on section 10, colour E on section 11 and colour F on section 12.

The strips on sections 1, 7, 13, 19, 25, 31 and 37 of this pattern are all of colour A. The strips on sections 2, 8, 14, 20, 26, 32 and 38 are all of colour B. The strips on sections 3, 9, 15, 21, 27, 33 and 39 are all of colour C. The strips on sections 4, 10, 16, 22, 28, 34 and 40 are all of colour D. The strips on sections 5, 11, 17, 23, 29, 35 and 41 are all of colour E. The strips on sections 6, 12, 18, 24, 30, 36 and 42 are all of colour F.

Finishing

Carefully remove the card after finishing section 42. Stick a piece of holographic paper in the middle on the back of the card. You can use punches, figure scissors and bits of paper to add extra finishing touches to the card. Stick small pieces of double-sided adhesive tape along the edges or use foam tape to bridge the height difference. Remove the protective layer from the double-sided adhesive tape and stick your design on a double card. Do not use glue, because all the paper strips place pressure on the card.

Embossing

To emboss, place the stencil on the good side of the card and stick it in place using masking tape. Place the card (with the stencil) upside-down on a light box and carefully push the paper through the stencil's opening using the embossing stylus. You only have to push along the edges to raise the entire image.
Rub the point of the embossing stylus with a candle so that it glides smoothly over the paper.

Materials

To make the cards:
- ❏ Card: Canson Mi-Teintes (C), Artoz (A) and Papicolor (P)
- ❏ Pergamano Parchment separating sheets
- ❏ Iris folding text stickers
- ❏ Iris folding greetings sheets
- ❏ Borders & Corners paper (Sharon Ann)
- ❏ Knife and cutting mat
- ❏ Ruler with a metal cutting edge (Securit)
- ❏ Adhesive tape
- ❏ Double-sided adhesive tape and foam tape
- ❏ Masking tape
- ❏ Various punches (Carl, Lim)
- ❏ Various corner punches (Fiskars, Lim, Reuser)

- ❏ Border ornament punches (Fiskars, Vaessen)
- ❏ Scissors and silhouette scissors
- ❏ Figure scissors (Fiskars)
- ❏ Hole punch
- ❏ Photo glue
- ❏ Pencil
- ❏ Light box

Iris folding
- ❏ Strips of used envelopes
- ❏ Strips of Iris folding paper
- ❏ Strips of de luxe Iris folding paper
- ❏ Strips of holographic paper (Em-Je)

The middle of the card
- ❏ Holographic paper

The patterns
Full-size examples of all the patterns are given in this book. Use a light box to draw round the outside. The shapes are usually easy to cut out of card. Specially punched cards are available for the wine glass, the pinecone, the Celtic star, the holly leaf and the hourglass.

Hexagons

All the cards are made according to the instructions given for the basic pattern (see Techniques).

Card 1 – Basic pattern

Card: pink A481 (14.8 x 21 cm), dark blue A417 (14 x 10 cm) and ice blue P42 (13 x 9.7 cm) • Pattern 1 • 2 cm wide strips from 2 blue envelopes and from 4 sheets of Iris folding paper (blue, red and de luxe pastels sets) • Silver holographic paper (Em-Je) • Spindle figure scissors • Arrow corner punch

Punch the corners of the smallest card and cut out the hexagon. After completing the Iris folding, cut the points for the ice-crystal. To do so, make an incision in the holographic paper with the figure scissors, turn the scissors over and then, approximately 0.5 cm away from the incision, cut upwards at an angle to produce a point.

Card 2

Card: pastel green A331 (14.8 x 21 cm), dark blue A417 (14 x 9.5 cm) and white (13.6 x 9.1 cm) • Pattern 1 • 6 groups of 2 cm wide strips from 4 sheets of Iris folding paper (blue, purple, petrol and de luxe pastels sets) • Silver holographic paper • Vulcano figure scissors • Snowflakes 3-in-1 corner punch

For the points, fold a strip of holographic paper double, cut it at an angle once with the figure scissors and once with normal scissors. Fold it open and stick it on the card.

Card 3

Card: white (14.8 x 21 cm) and light blue C490 (14.8 x 9.2 cm) • Pattern 1 • 6 groups of 2 cm wide strips from 3 blue envelopes and from 2 Iris folding sheets (blue and petrol sets) • Silver holographic paper • Bells border picture punch

Card 4

Card: indigo C140 (14.8 x 21 cm) and white (13.8 x 10 cm) • Pattern 1 • 2 cm wide strips from 5 blue envelopes and from 1 sheet of Iris folding paper (blue set) • Silver holographic paper • Heartstrings figure scissors • Star border ornament punch

Card 5

Card: azure A393 (13 x 26 cm), night blue P41 (12 x 12 cm) and Stars silver holographic paper

1.

2.

3.

4.

5.

6.

7.

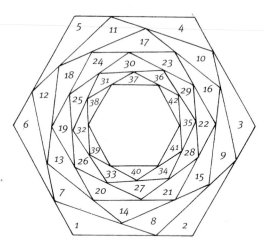

Pattern 1 – Basic shape

wide strips from 4 envelopes (pink, blue and grey) • Silver Holographic paper • Heartbeat figure scissors

Card 7

Card: azure P04 (14.8 x 21 cm) and metallic white (13.8 x 9.7 cm) • Pattern 1 • 2 cm wide strips from 2 envelopes (grey and blue) and from 3 sheets of Iris folding paper (de luxe colourful and pastels sets and a Christmas Iris folding greetings sheet) • Superstencil MD SU 4002 • Silver thread • Silver holographic paper Prick the embroidery cardboard. Emboss the edges and cut the hexagon out of the white card. Embroider the diamond pattern and fill the ice-crystal with strips.

(12.3 x 12.3 cm) • Pattern 1 • 6 groups of 2 cm wide strips from 1 blue envelope and from 5 sheets of Iris folding paper (aqua set) • Silver holographic paper • Seagull figure scissors • Snowflakes 3-in-1 corner punch

Card 6

Card: white (13 x 26 cm and 10 x 10 cm) • Dotted parchment 1643 (12 x 12 cm) and lavender blue 1602 (11 x 11 cm) • Pattern 1 • 6 groups of 2 cm

Playing with hexagons

Cheers!

The cognac glass is made according to the instructions given for card 1. Note: whilst Iris folding, the hexagon will change into a square.

Card 1

Card: mango P40 (13 x 26 cm), metallic golden brown P144 (11.5 x 11.5 cm), brick red P35 (11.1 x 11.1 cm) and light beige C340 (10.5 x 10.5 cm) • Pattern 2 • 6 groups of 2 cm wide strips from 5 sheets of Iris folding paper

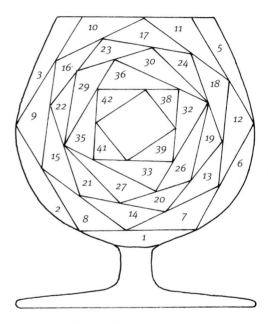

Pattern 2 – Cognac glass

(orange, yellow and de luxe pastels sets) • Bronze holographic paper
Cut the goblet, without the stem and the foot, out of the smallest card. Use a light box to copy the stem and the foot onto a strip of brown Iris

folding paper. Cut it out and stick it below the goblet. To avoid making a mistake, read these instructions first and use 6 coloured pencils to mark the sections of your copy of the pattern with the correct colours. Colour D (pink) is not included in the first round of Iris folding. Colour A (dark brown) will be in sections 1, 7, 13 and 19 and will then stop. There are no sections 25, 31 and 37. Colour D (pink) will be in sections 10, 16, and 22 and will then stop. There are no sections 4, 28, 34 and 40. Once a colour is no longer going to be used, remove the strips from the table and continue with the other colours.

Card 2

Card: dark brown P38 (13 x 26 cm), metallic golden brown P144 (12 x 12 cm) and white (11 x 11 cm) • Pattern 2 • 2 cm wide strips from 2 brown envelopes and from 4 sheets of Iris folding paper (yellow, red and de luxe Christmas sets) • Bronze holographic paper • Regal corner scissors

Card 3

Card: dark brown (13 x 26 cm), gold P102 (11.6 x 11.6 cm) and white C335 (10.7 x 10.7 cm) • Pattern 2 • 2 cm wide strips from 1 cloudy

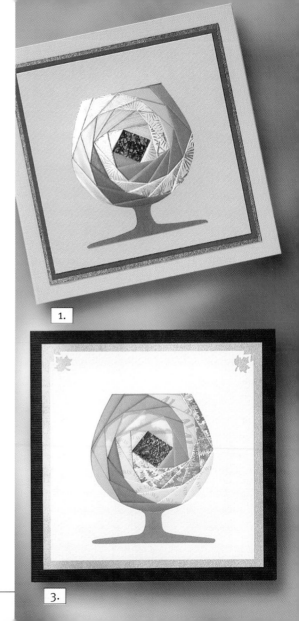

1.

3.

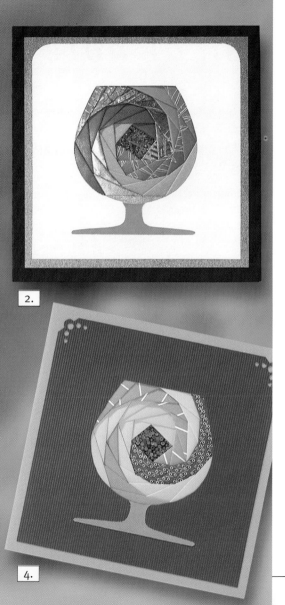

2.

4.

envelope and from 5 sheets of Iris folding paper (yellow, orange and red sets) • Gold holographic paper • Leaves 3-in-1 corner punch Punch the top corners of the white card and cut out the goblet.

Card 4
Card: salmon beige C384 (13 x 26 cm) and rust (12 x 12 cm) • Pattern 2 • 2 cm wide strips from 6 beige/brown envelopes • Gold holographic paper • Reuser multi corner punch Punch the top corners of the rust card and cut out the goblet.

Guitar and musical note

Music gives colour to your life.

The guitar is made according to the description given for card 1 and the musical note is made according to the description given for card 5.

Card 1

Card: caramel P26 (14.8 x 21 cm), metallic golden brown P144 (14 x 9.6 cm) and white (14 x 6.7 cm) • Pattern 3 • 2 cm wide strips from 4 sheets of Iris folding paper (orange and yellow sets) • Gold holographic paper • Musical notes border punch

Cut the guitar, without the stem, out of the white card. Note: colour A (bronze) stops after section 21b. There are no sections 25 and 29. For colour B (brown), there is no section 22, nor section 30, but there is a section 26. Copy half of the ring and half of the stem onto a strip of colour B. Fold them double and cut them out. Stick the ring in the middle and stick the stem over the ring. Punch the edges of the brown card.

Card 2

Card: petrol (14.8 x 21 cm) and white (14.3 x 9 cm) • Pattern 3 • 4 groups of 2 cm wide strips from 2 green envelopes and from 2 sheets of Iris folding paper (petrol set) • Silver holographic paper • Music multi corner punch

Card 3

Card: pale yellow P29 (14.8 x 21 cm) and nut brown P39 (14.8 x 8 cm) • Pattern 3 • 2 cm wide strips from 2 brown envelopes and from 2 sheets of Iris folding paper (orange and de luxe pastels sets) • Gold holographic paper • Decorations from a Music multi corner punch

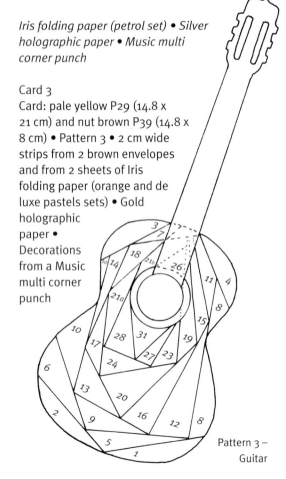

Pattern 3 –
Guitar

Card 4

Card: brick red C130 (14.8 x 21 cm) and white (13.7 x 10 cm) • Sheet of burgundy Iris folding paper from the red set (14.2 x 10 cm) • Pattern 3 • 2 cm wide strips from 4 sheets of Iris folding paper (Avec set) • Silver holographic paper
Cut a strip of 6 x 3.5 cm and a strip of 7 x 4 cm off of the white card.

Card 5

Card: gold line P301 (14.8 x 21 cm) and brick red C130 (13.3 x 9.1 cm) • Pattern 4 • 2 cm wide strips from 1 brown envelope, from 1 sheet of music paper and from 2 sheets of Iris folding paper (purple and de luxe pastels sets) • De luxe Iris folding paper (7 x 3.5 cm) for the stem • Music paper (13.3 x 1 cm) • Bronze holographic paper
Cut out the circle from the note and fill it with strips.

Card 6

Card: Structura cherry red P133 (14.8 x 21 cm) and metallic white (13 x 8.8 cm) • Stars holographic paper (13.5 x 9.3 cm) • Pattern 4 • 2 cm wide strips from 2 red envelopes and from 2 grey envelopes • Red paper (7 x 3.5 cm) for the stem • Stars holographic paper

Card 7

Card: dark green A309 (14.8 x 21 cm) and pastel green A331 (13.3 x 9 cm) • Pattern 4 • 2 cm wide strips from 2 envelopes (purple and green) and from 2 sheets of Iris folding paper (petrol and de luxe pastels sets) • Purple paper (7 x 3.5 cm) for the stem • Silver holographic paper • Music border punch

Card 8

Card: grey C431 (14.8 x 21 cm), bright red C506 (14 x 10 cm) and white (13.7 x 9.5 cm) • Pattern 4 • 2 cm wide strips from 4 grey and dark blue envelopes • Grey paper (7 x 3.5 cm) for the stem • Silver holographic paper • Accolade corner punch • Musical note figure punch

Pattern 4 – Musical note

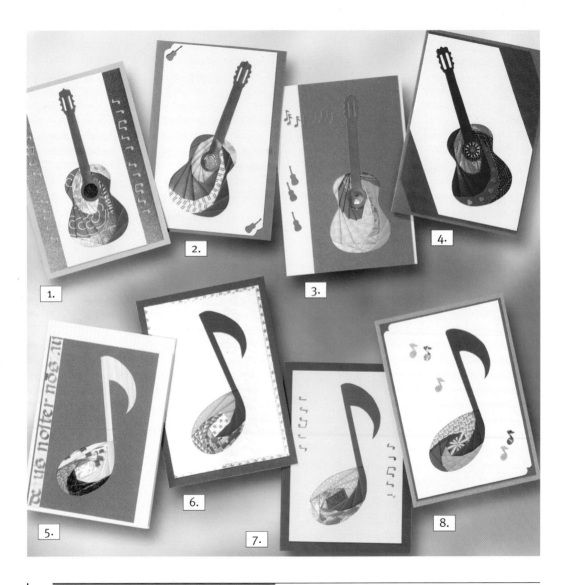

1.

2.

3.

4.

5.

6.

7.

8.

Flags and sweets

Let's celebrate!

The flags are made according to the description given for card 1 and the sweets are made according to the description given for card 5.

Card 1
Card: pastel blue A413 (14.8 x 21 cm), corn-flower A425 (13.8 x 9.5 cm) and sky blue A391 (13.3 x 9 cm) • Pattern 5 • 1.5 cm wide strips from 3 sheets of Iris folding paper (blue and purple sets) • Silver holographic paper • Flowers 3-in-1 corner punch • Hole punch for the top of the flag pole
Cut the flags, without the poles, out of the smallest card.

Card 2
Card: white (14.8 x 21 cm and 9.7 x 7.5 cm) and fiesta red P12 (13 x 9.7 cm) • Hearts vellum (Heyda) (11.5 x 9.1 cm) • Pattern 5 • 1.5 cm wide strips from 3 sheets of Iris folding paper (green and de luxe flowers sets) • Silver holographic paper • Girl figure punch • Hole punch

Card 3
Card: Structura pale yellow P132 (14.8 x 21 cm), iris blue P31 (14 x 9.8 cm) and spring green P08 (13.6 x 8.6 cm) • 2 strips (13.6 x 1 cm) from a blue Iris folding greetings sheet • Pattern 5 • 1.5 cm wide strips from 2 envelopes (blue and green) and from 1 sheet of Iris folding paper (blue set) • Silver holographic paper • Hearts from a heart border ornament punch • Hole punch

Card 4
Card: white (14.8 x 21 cm) and fiesta red P12 (10.8 x 8.4 cm) • Sweet vellum (Heyda) (14.8 x 21 cm) • Pattern 5 • 3 groups of 1.5 cm

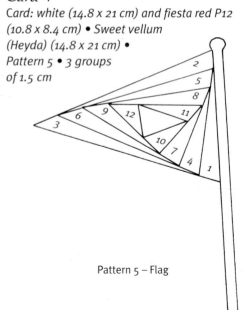

Pattern 5 – Flag

wide strips from 2 red envelopes and from a red Iris folding greetings sheet • Number 4 from Juliana Die-Cut Alphabet • Silver holographic paper • Hole punch

Card 5

Card: pine green A339 (14.8 x 21 cm), Structura fern green P137 (12.5 x 8.3 cm) and white (14 x 9.5 cm and 10.7 x 7.5 cm) • Pattern 6 • 1.5 cm wide strips from 4 sheets of Iris folding paper (green and yellow sets) • 2 pieces of green Iris folding paper (3 x 3 cm) for the bows • Green holographic paper • Multi corner punch
Punch two corners of each single card and cut the sweet, without the bows, out of the smallest card. Use a light box to copy the bows.

Card 6

Card: Structura sunflower P134 (14.8 x 21 cm) and white (13.8 x 9.5 cm) • Orange Iris folding paper (14.2 x 9.8 cm) • Pattern 6 • 1.5 cm wide strips from 4 yellow and 4 orange envelopes • 4 pieces of envelope paper (3 x 3 cm) • Gold holographic paper • Fountain corner punch

Card 7

Card: mango A575 (14.8 x 21 cm), bright orange

(14.2 x 9.8 cm) and white (13.5 x 9.5 cm) • Pattern 6 • 4 groups of 1.5 cm wide strips from 2 red envelopes and from 2 sheets of Iris folding paper (red set) • 4 pieces of red paper • Rainbow holographic paper • Multi corner punch

Card 8

Card: violet P20 (14.8 x 21 cm), cornflower A425 (13.8 x 9.5 cm) and white (12.8 x 8.5 cm) • Pattern 6 • 1.5 cm wide strips from 4 purple envelopes • 2 pieces of paper (3 x 3 cm) • Silver holographic paper • Hearts 3-in-1 corner punch

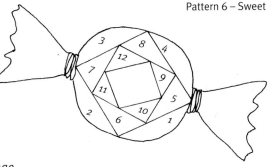

Pattern 6 – Sweet

Celtic star

A chic star.

All the cards are made according to the instructions given for card 1.

Card 1 (card on the cover)
Card: azure P04 (13 x 26 cm), white (12 x 12 cm) and dark blue P06 (11.7 x 11.7 cm) • Pattern 7 • 2 cm wide strips from 3 envelopes (yellow, grey and blue) and from 1 sheet of Iris folding paper (aqua set) • Silver holographic paper • Celestial 3-in-1 corner punch
Punch the corners of the smallest card and cut out the four points of the star. First, cover the striped sections around the middle with the yellow strips and then use the other three colours for the Iris folding. Cut a yellow circle (Ø 1.7 cm) and stick it on the front of the card.

Card 2
Card: dark blue A417 (13 x 26 cm) and white (11.3 x 11.3 cm) • Pattern 7 • 2 cm wide strips from 1 green envelope and from 3 sheets of Iris folding paper (petrol and de luxe colourful sets) • Silver holographic paper • Lily corner punch (Carl)
Punch the corners of the white card.

1.

Fijne
Feestdagen

3.

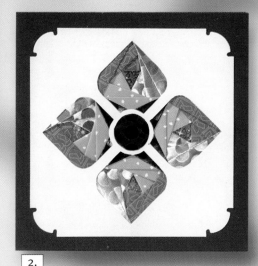

2.

Card 3

Card: white (13 x 26 cm and 11 x 11 cm) and purple P46 (11.9 x 11.9 cm) • Pattern 7 • 2 cm wide strips from 4 sheets of Iris folding paper (red and purple sets) • Gold holographic paper • Iris folding text sticker

When you have finished the Iris folding, stick a red circle in the middle.

Card 4

Card: Structura pale yellow P132 (13 x 26 cm), honey yellow A243 (11.8 x 11.8 cm) and night blue P41 (11.8 x 11.8 cm) • Pattern 7 • 2 cm wide strips from 3 yellow envelopes and from 1 sheet of Iris folding paper (de luxe Christmas set) • Gold stars holographic paper • Star corner punch

Use the gold paper to cover the striped sections in the middle. Also use it to make the circle in the middle.

4.

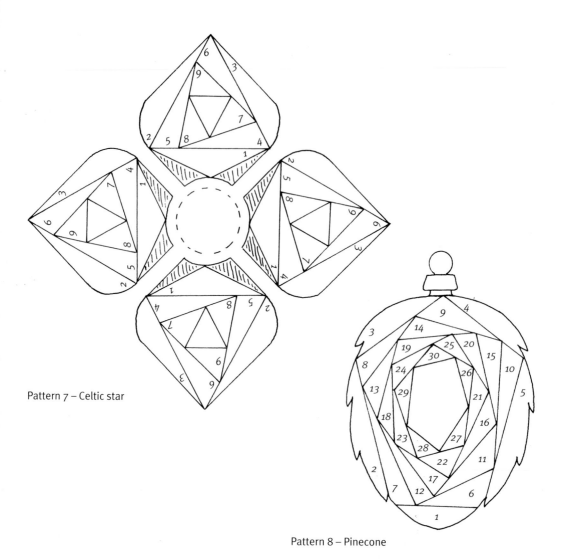

Pattern 7 – Celtic star

Pattern 8 – Pinecone

Pinecone and holly

The pinecones are made according to the description given for card 1 and the holly leaves are made according to the description given for card 2.

Card 1 (card on the cover)

Card: dark green A309 (14.8 x 21 cm) and white (13.8 x 9.5 cm) • Pattern 8 • 2 cm wide strips from 4 sheets of Iris folding paper (petrol and aqua sets) • Silver holographic paper • Accolade corner punch

Punch the corners of the white card. Cut out the pinecone without the suspension eye. After finishing the Iris folding, cut the suspension eye out of holographic paper and stick it on the card.

Card 2

Card: mint green (14.8 x 21 cm), metallic emerald P143 (13.2 x 9.5 cm) and white (12 x 8.5 cm) • Pattern 9 • 5 groups of 2 cm wide strips from 2 green envelopes and from 2 sheets of Iris folding paper (petrol and green sets) • Silver holographic paper • Berries from a hole punch • Holly corner punch

Punch the corners of the white card and cut out the leaf without the stem. After finishing the Iris folding, cut out the stem and stick it on the card together with the berries.

Card 3

Card: dark green A309 (13 x 26 cm), pastel green A331 (10.6 x 10.6 cm), dark blue A417 (10 x 10 cm), metallic emerald P143 (9.1 x 9.1 cm) and white (8.5 x 8.5 cm) • Pattern 8 • 5 groups of 2 cm wide strips from 1 turquoise envelope and from 3 sheets of Iris folding paper (petrol and de luxe pastels sets) • Silver holographic paper

Card 4

Card: Christmas green P18 (14.8 x 21 cm), silvery grey (13.8 x 9.3 cm) and white (13 x 8.5 cm) • Pattern 9 • 5 groups of 2 cm wide strips from 4 sheets of Iris folding paper (blue and petrol sets) • Piece of Iris folding paper (5 x 8 cm – petrol set) for the second leaf • Silver holographic paper

Card 5

Card: cerise P33 (14.8 x 21 cm), burgundy (13.8 x 10 cm) and metallic white (12.8 x 9 cm) • Pattern 8 • 2 cm wide strips from 2 sheets of holographic paper (stars and holly) and from 3 sheets of Iris folding paper (red and purple sets) • Silver holographic paper • Bow border picture punch

Card 6

Card: white (14.8 x 21 cm and 11 x 6.7 cm), Perla gold P141 (12.9 x 8.7 cm) and red (12.3 x 8 cm) • Pattern 9 • 5 groups of 2 cm wide strips from 4 sheets of Iris folding paper (petrol and green sets) • Hole punch • Gold holographic paper

Card 7

Card: ivory C111 (13 x 26 cm and 8 x 8 cm) and brick red P35 (11 x 11 cm) • Piece of Iris folding paper (11.4 x 11.4 cm – green set) • Pattern 9 • 5 groups of 2 cm wide strips from 1 red envelope, from 1 beige envelope and from 2 sheets of Iris folding paper (green set) • Hole punch • Gold holographic paper

Card 8

Card: brick red P35 (14.8 x 21 cm) and ivory C111 (13.7 x 9.5 cm) • Pattern 8 • 2 cm wide strips from 1 orange envelope and from 4 sheets of Iris folding paper (yellow and orange sets) • 2 strips of 9.5 cm Borders & Corners Oak Leaf/Plaid paper • Gold holographic paper

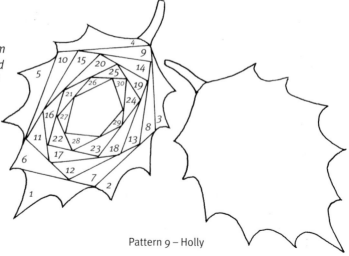

Pattern 9 – Holly

1.

2.

3.

4.

5.

6.

7.

8.

Pumpkins

Why don't you make a

Halloween card?

All the cards are made according to the instructions given for card 1.

Card 1

Card: mango A575 (13 x 26 cm), iris blue P31 (12.6 x 12.6 cm) and metallic golden brown P144 (11 x 11 cm) • Dotted parchment 1643 (12.2 x 12.2 cm) • Pattern 10 • 2.5 cm wide strips from 6 sheets of Iris folding paper (orange, purple and green sets) • 2 pieces of paper (7 x 4 cm) for the sides and 1 piece of gold paper (3 x 4 cm) for the stem • Witch figure punch • Celestial 3-in-1 corner punch

Cut the pumpkin, without the stem and the sides, out of the smallest card. Read these instructions first and then colour the sections on the copy of the pumpkin pattern using coloured pencils. Note: colour A (purple) is not used after section 25 and there are no sections 31 and 37. Colour C (pink) is not used after section 27 and there are no sections 33 and 39. Colour E (brown) is not used after section 29 and there are no sections 35 and 41. After section 30, you only continue with colours B, D and F. Cut the top edge of strip 34b using the figure scissors and stick eyes on strips 38 and 42. After finishing the Iris folding, use a light box to copy the sides and the stem. Cut them out and stick them on the front of the card.

Card 2

Card: pastel green A331 (13 x 26 cm), lemon P09 (12.2 x 12.2 cm) and sea green (12 x 12 cm) • Pattern 10 • 2.5 cm wide strips from 1 green envelope and from 5 sheets of Iris folding paper (yellow and green sets) • Green paper (two pieces 7 x 4 cm and one piece 3 x 4 cm) • Gold holographic paper • Iris folding text sticker • Star figure punches • Arrow corner punch

Card 3

Card: wine red P36 (13 x 26 cm) and Structura orange P135 (11 x 11 cm) • Iris folding paper (11.3 x 11.3 cm - de luxe flowers set) • Pattern 10 • 6 groups of 2.5 cm wide strips from 4 sheets of Iris folding paper (red, yellow and de luxe flowers sets) • Red Iris folding paper (7 x 8 cm) • Rainbow holographic paper • Accolade corner punch • Star punch

Card 4

Card: fawn A241 (13 x 26 cm), grey blue C354

(12.2 x 12.2 cm) and wine red P36 (11.5 x 12 cm)
• Pattern 10 • 6 groups of 2.5 cm strips from 5
envelopes (ochre, beige, grey and burgundy)
and from 1 sheet of Iris folding paper (green set)
• Ochre paper (7 x 8 cm) • 2 strips of Borders &
Corners Pine/Gingham paper (12 x 0.6 cm) • Gold
holographic paper • Mini shell figure scissors

Card 5
Card: lobster red A545 (13 x 26 cm), gold P300
(12 x 12 cm), crimson A549 (11.5 x 11.5 cm) and
white (11 x 11 cm) • Pattern 10 • 6 groups of
2.5 cm wide strips from 1 yellow envelope and
from 4 sheets of Iris folding paper (orange and
yellow sets) • Orange paper (7 x 8 cm) •
Gold holographic paper • Borders and
Corners Red Oak paper

Card 6
Card: black A219 (13 x 26 cm) and
olive green P45 (11 x 11 cm) • Lime
green Fantasy parchment 1600
(12.5 x 12.5 cm) and light green paper
(11.6 x 11.6 cm) • Pattern 10 • 2.5 cm
wide strips from 6 sheets of Iris folding
paper (green set) • Green paper (7 x 8
cm) • Green holographic paper • Celestial
3-in-1 corner punch

Card 7
Card: gold line P301 (13 x 26 cm) and cognac
brown (10 x 10 cm) • Pale yellow parchment
1645 (12 x 12 cm) • Pattern 10 • 6 groups of
2.5 cm wide strips from 5 sheets of Iris folding
paper (yellow and green sets) • Gold paper
(7 x 8 cm) • Gold holographic paper
• Heartbeat figure scissors •
Witch figure punch

Pattern 10 – Pumpkin

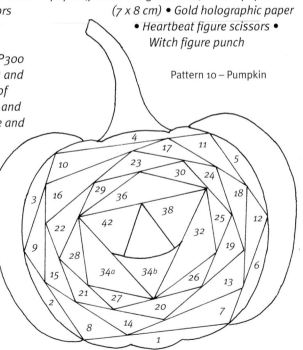

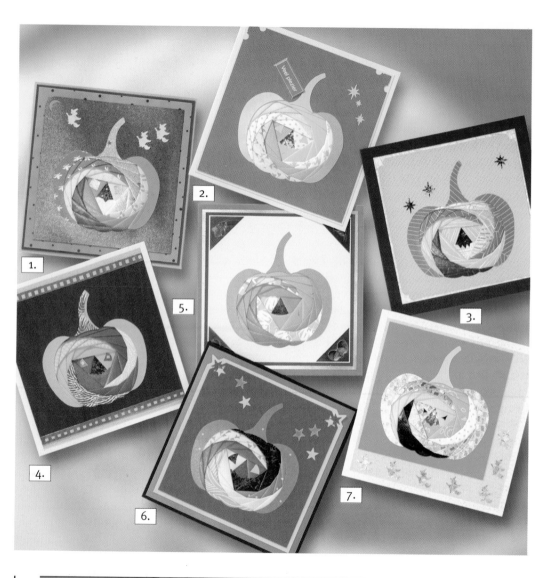

1.

2.

3.

4.

5.

6.

Hourglass and wine glass

Best wishes!

is made according to the description given for card 4.

The hourglass is made according to the description given for card 1. The wine glass

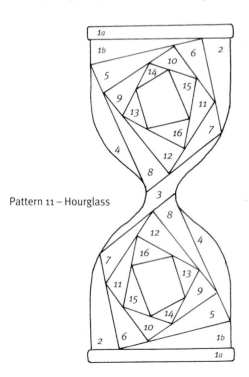

Pattern 11 – Hourglass

Card 1

Card: white (14.8 x 21 cm) and wine red (14.2 x 10 cm - 120 gram) • Pattern 11 • 2 cm wide strips from 4 beige/white envelopes • Gold holographic paper • Asiatic symbol punch
Turn the punch upside down and punch all the corners of the red paper twice with part of the pattern. Use a copy of the pattern to copy the hourglass and cut it out.

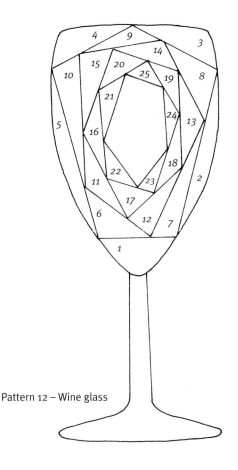

Pattern 12 – Wine glass

Card 2

Card: night blue P41 (14.8 x 21 cm), ice blue P42 (14.2 x 10 cm) and white (13 x 8.5 cm) • Pattern 11 • 2 cm wide strips from 4 sheets of Iris folding paper (aqua, blue and de luxe pastels sets) • Silver holographic paper • Fountain corner punch

After punching the card, stick pieces of holographic paper behind the fountains.

Card 3

Card: red (14.8 x 21 cm), mustard yellow P48 (13.9 x 9.3 cm) and cream P27 (13 x 8.5 cm) • Pattern 11 • 2 cm wide strips from 3 envelopes (grey, bronze and burgundy) and from 1 sheet of Iris folding paper (de luxe pastels set) • Gold holographic paper • Borders and Corners Red Oak paper

Card 4

Card: white (14.8 x 21 cm and 13.5 x 9.1 cm), Christmas red P43 (14.2 x 9.9 cm) and metallic aubergine P146 (14 x 9.7 cm) • Pattern 12 • 5 groups of 2 cm wide strips from 2 red envelopes, from 1 sheet of Iris folding paper (de luxe flowers) and from 1 red Iris folding greetings sheet • Red paper (5 x 5 cm) for the stem • Silver holographic paper • Leaf mini punch

Cut the glass out of the white card. After finishing the Iris folding, stick the stem and the leaves on the front of the card.

Card 5

Card: orange P11 (14.8 x 21 cm), Perla golden yellow P141 (14.3 x 10 cm) and lemon C101 (13.8 x 9.5 cm) • Pattern 12 • 5 groups of 2 cm wide strips from 1 yellow envelope and from 3 sheets of Iris folding paper (yellow, orange and de luxe flowers sets) • Yellow paper (5 x 5 cm)

• Gold holographic paper • Iris folding text sticker • Fountain corner punch

Card 6

Card: heather P22 (14.8 x 21 cm) and Christmas red P43 (13.4 x 8.9 cm) • Pattern 12 • 5 groups of 2 cm wide strips from 1 pink envelope and from 3 sheets of Iris folding paper (orange, red and de luxe colourful sets) • Pink paper (5 x 5 cm) • Silver holographic paper • Star border ornament punch

Many thanks to

Kars & Co BV in Ochten, the Netherlands
Em-Je B.V. in Zuidwolde, the Netherlands
Pergamano International in Uithoorn, the Netherlands

The materials used can be ordered by shopkeepers from:
Kars & Co BV in Ochten, the Netherlands.
Papicolor International in Utrecht, the Netherlands.
Em-Je B.V. in Zuidwolde, the Netherlands
Pergamano International in Uithoorn, the Netherlands